16

FRED FLINTSTONE'S ADVENTURES with WHEELS and AXLES

Bedrock and Roll!

by Mark Weakland

illustrated by Alan Brown

CAPSTONE PRESS
a capstone imprint

Every morning Barney and I drive to work. I'm glad a smart caveman invented the wheel and axle. Without them this car would sit here like a rock. Together a wheel and axle are a simple machine. Other simple machines include the wedge, pulley, inclined plane, lever, and screw. Come on, Barney! Let's roll! We don't want to be late for work.

Two wheels on a motorcycle help people get back and forth to work.

Here at the quarry, Mr. Slate gives us a lot of work to do. But the wheels and axles on these wheelbarrows make our work easier. The wheel turns around the axle. Together a wheel and axle help us do work while using less effort. Now that's the Fred Flintstone style!

Wheels on a dump truck make it easy to move tons of earth and rock.

Let me tell you about wheels and friction, Barney. Friction is a force that slows down motion. It happens when two things rub together or slide past each other.

Sure, Fred.

Just look at the poor dino! It's working hard to overcome friction. But the second one isn't working as hard. That's because wheels reduce friction.

Rocko's cart also helps make work easier to do. The cart and our wheelbarrows have wheels. The wheels cut down on friction when we move the rocks. When Rocko uses a cart, he doesn't have to work as hard.

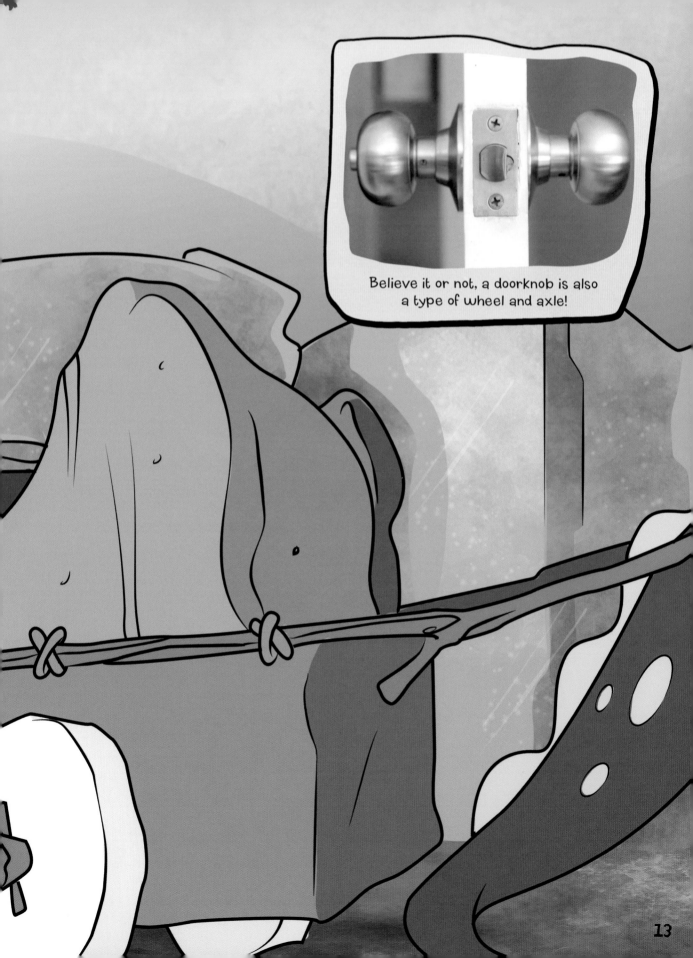

Believe it or not, a doorknob is also
a type of wheel and axle!

Big wheels enable tractors to do lots of difficult farm work.

Wheels move us back and forth to work. They roll us down the driveway. They even give us a lift, especially when we step on them! But gravity always brings us back down. Wilma! Who left the roller skates lying around?

Wheels can be found on all types of fun things, such as this skateboard.

Glossary

axle—a bar in the center of a wheel around which a wheel turns

effort—the force applied to a machine to do work

force—a push or pull exerted upon an object

friction—a force produced when two objects rub against each other; friction slows down objects

gravity—a force that pulls objects together

load—an object that moves when a force is applied

quarry—a place where stone or other minerals are dug from the ground

reduce—to make something smaller or less in amount or size

valve—a movable part that controls the flow of liquid or gas through a pipe

Read More

Bailey, Gerry. *Rolling Along: The Wheel and Axle.* The Robotx Get Help from Simple Machines. New York: Crabtree Publishing Company, 2014.

LaMachia, Dawn. *Wheels and Anxles at Work.* Zoom in on Simple Machines. New York: Enslow Publishing, 2016.

Oxlade, Chris. *Making Machines with Wheels and Axles.* Simple Machine Projects. Chicago: Capstone Raintree, 2015.

Internet Sites

FactHound offers a safe, fun way to find Internet sites related to this book. All of the sites on FactHound have been researched by our staff.

Here's all you do:

Visit *www.facthound.com*

Type in this code: 9781491484746

Super-cool stuff!

Check out projects, games and lots more at
www.capstonekids.com

Index

Look for all the books in the series:

Thanks to our adviser for his expertise, research, and advice:
Paul Ohmann, PhD, Associate Professor of Physics
University of St. Thomas, St. Paul, Minnesota

Published in 2016 by Capstone Press, A Capstone Imprint
1710 Roe Crest Drive, North Mankato, Minnesota 56003
www.mycapstone.com

Library of Congress Cataloging-in-Publication Data
Weakland, Mark, author.
  Fred Flintstone's adventures with wheels and axles : Bedrock and roll! / by Mark Weakland ; illustrated by Alan Brown.
  pages cm — (Flintstones explain simple machines)
Summary: "Popular cartoon character Fred Flintstone explains how wheels and axles work and how he uses simple machines in his daily life"—Provided by publisher.
Audience: 6–8.
Audience: K to grade 3.
ISBN 978-1-4914-8474-6 (library binding)
ISBN 978-1-4914-8480-7 (eBook PDF)
1. Wheels—Juvenile literature. 2. Axles—Juvenile literature. 3. Simple machines—Juvenile literature. I. Brown, Alan (Graphic designer), illustrator. II. Title. III. Title: Adventures with wheels and axles. IV. Series: Weakland, Mark. Flintstones explain simple machines.
TJ181.5.W423 2016
621.8—dc23   2015024737

Editorial Credits
Editor: Alesha Halvorson
Designer: Ashlee Suker
Creative Director: Nathan Gassman
Media Researcher: Tracy Cummins
Production Specialist: Kathy McColley

The illustrations in this book were created digitally.

Image Credits
Shutterstock: dragunov, 9, oticki, 15, pudiq, 5, wittaya loysoungsin, 13; Thinkstock: Corepics VOF, 20, M_Arnold, 17

Printed in the United States of America in
North Mankato, MN. 092015 009221CGS16